ANTHROPOLOGICAL PAPERS

MUSEUM OF ANTHROPOLOGY, UNIVERSITY OF MICHIGAN

NO. 12

The Chronological Position of the Hopewellian Culture in the Eastern United States

by
JAMES B. GRIFFIN

ANN ARBOR
UNIVERSITY OF MICHIGAN, 1958

© 1958 by the Regents of the University of Michigan
The Museum of Anthropology
All rights reserved

ISBN (print): 978-1-949098-31-0
ISBN (ebook): 978-1-951519-55-1

Browse all of our books at
sites.lsa.umich.edu/archaeology-books.

Order our books from the University of Michigan
Press at www.press.umich.edu.

For permissions, questions, or manuscript queries,
contact Museum publications by email at umma-
pubs@umich.edu or visit the Museum website at
lsa.umich.edu/ummaa.

CONTENTS

	Page
Introduction.	1
Adena Complex	2
Ohio Hopewell	5
Northeastern Point Peninsula and Early Woodland Dates	8
Illinois Hopewell Dates	11
Northern Hopewell and Late Woodland Dates	16
Hopewell Dates from Central and Western Missouri	19
The Dating Problem in the Lower Mississippi Valley	22
Literature Cited	25

INTRODUCTION

This paper[1] presents a rather large series of radiocarbon dates which bear upon the origin, age, and disappearance of the Hopewellian complex (see Figures 1 and 2). At this time I shall not define the Hopewellian complex, but will depend upon my readers to have, or obtain, a general idea of its major characteristics as detailed in the several chapters in a previous publication (Griffin, 1952c). For many years in the 1800's and early 1900's archaeologists were unable to propose satisfactory theories for the origin of what was then regarded as a rich and varied archaeological complex which suddenly appeared in Ohio without antecedents and which disappeared without a trace. Clear recognition of the wide areal distribution of the Hopewellian complex is a product of the last thirty years or so. Increasing attention to temporal differences in the various regions which it occupied has provided significant antecedents of many traits and trait complexes which become intensified in Hopewellian. In some areas a gradual shift from Hopewellian tradition and styles may be seen and new culture types and stages take their place. The addition of radiocarbon dating to the archaeologists' repertoire of interpretive techniques has aided in the solution of some problems but has raised others of striking proportions.

One of the most important developments, as a result of radiocarbon dates, was to provide a long period for the growth, spread, and decline of the Hopewellian, in contrast to the two hundred years or so which was suggested as a reasonable time span by archaeologists in the 1930's. The temporal allocation of Hopewellian in the north, from about 400 B.C. to A.D. 400, places it on a time level that means that it is by far the most highly developed and sophisticated prehistoric complex north of the Rio Grande and that the Ohio to Lower Missouri Valley area was a dominant culture center. The importance of this center is perhaps a reason for the influx of the exotic raw materials from the northern, eastern, and southern margins of the United States and from the Plains and Rocky Mountain area to the west. While no recent assay has been made of the number and diversity of Hopewell sites in Ohio, investigations in Illinois and Missouri have increased the number known from a score or so to up into the hundreds.

Some archaeologists of the past and present generations have explained the appearance of Hopewell traits in such widely separated

---

[1] Read at the American Anthropological Association meeting in Chicago, December, 1957.

areas as Michigan, Indiana, Illinois, Wisconsin, and Louisiana and Florida as either due to establishment of trading posts of Ohio Hopewell or as resulting from a migration of Hopewell people from Ohio to such distant lands. Some recent archaeological interpretations have migrated Adena from Mexico or South America, or have explained Ohio Hopewell as a migration from Louisiana, or even Siberia. The known time span of Hopewellian and the increasing evidence of a gradual cultural development, which differed in various geographic regions, have made all the migration theories obsolete. This is not to deny that culture spreads or develops only through the behavior of people; I recognize that cultural elements are not spread overland by crows or carried downstream by logs. There is considerable evidence of intimate exchange of ideas and materials over wide areas during the Hopewellian time span. While the exact mechanisms by which this took place are not too clearly known, in some instances hypotheses can be advanced.

The radiocarbon dates which are employed in this paper are those in Libby, 1955; Crane, 1956; Ford and Webb, 1956; and Crane and Griffin (1958a and b). They are based on assays made in five different laboratories by different techniques.[2] The samples were gathered by many individuals over a long period of time, in strikingly different environments, and with varying attention to collection and preservation. The samples, which are of different kinds of organic materials, vary in their reliability. Different runs on the same specimen that have given results far outside allowable statistical error tend to shake the faith of the social scientist or humanist in the magic of atomic science.

ADENA COMPLEX

The Adena complex of the central Ohio Valley is generally regarded as the first Woodland group in that area to construct burial mounds, and, perhaps, the first to have grown agricultural crops—of which corn was the primary staple. For some years it has been suggested that while Adena begins at a simple Early Woodland level it also lasts as a recognizably distinctive culture type into a period when Hopewell artifacts are being produced. At no time during the growth in complexity of Adena culture can it be said that there is evidence for a strong infusion of new traits which require a migration to account for them. Adena culture developed in the Ohio Valley and some of its characteristic traits are diffused from thence into adjoining states. Furthermore, Adena clearly represents the

---

[2] The laboratory responsible for each date is usually identified by a letter designation, for example: C-, University of Chicago; M-, University of Michigan; H-, Humble Oil Company; L-, Lamont, Columbia University.

basis for many of the cultural practices and concepts of Ohio Hopewell. The first radiocarbon dates on Adena sites were disturbing because they dated the mounds at A.D. 450 to 800. Some archaeologists impressed with "science," thought they could reverse the seriation of Adena-Hopewell traits; others argued that there was little connection between Adena and Hopewell; and still others implied that the archaeologists working with Ohio Valley prehistory were obviously not doing a good job of interpreting the cultural evidence.

Fourteen dates from Adena sites are now available and they confirm rather than refute the interpretation of both close and myopic students of the Adena complex. The first run on an Adena site was C-126 on bark preserved by contact with a copper reel-shaped breast plate in association with burial No. 7. The burial group was lying at the bottom of a pit, which was the central feature of the Drake Mound, Fayette County, Kentucky (Webb, Carey, and Snow, 1941). The date reported by Libby was A.D. 782±150. Prepared charcoal from this sample was submitted by Libby to the University of Michigan, where it was run as M-19 and dated 250 B.C. ±250. Webb informed me that he believed the Drake Mound to be late Adena (Griffin, 1951). This hypothesis was probably not based on his ingenious seriation of reel-shaped gorgets in which the copper gorget from the Drake Mound is one of the beginning forms of Adena reel-shaped gorgets (Webb, Carey, and Snow, 1941, p. 206).

The second Adena site dated was the Cowan Creek Mound in Clinton County, 6 miles south of Wilmington, Ohio. This mound was dug by Robert Goslin and Raymond S. Baby (Baby, 1949) of the Ohio State Museum. Charcoal from a subfloor fireplace just outside the house structure was dated as C-214 at A.D. 441±250. Since there has not been a full publication on this site, the meaning of this date is difficult to interpret. Underneath the mound, however, was a paired post-hole pattern of a circular house 45 feet in diameter. Of particular interest is the fact that a small fragment of either a cultivated gourd or pumpkin was found with the material. This is the first definite evidence of the existence of agriculture in an Adena mound site. The specimen was first examined by Volney H. Jones and later studied by Dr. Hugh C. Cutler and Dr. T. W. Whittaker in the Museum of Anthropology at the University of Michigan.

Two dates from the University of Chicago laboratory are on materials from an Adena mound at Dover in Mason County, Kentucky. Their first sample, C-759, was dated at 700 B.C. ±170, and the charcoal on which this run was made came from a large, heavily burned area near the top of the mound core. The second sample, from this same mound, was on charcoal associated with burial No. 55, which was a redeposited cremation near the mound base. Outside the skirt of the mound core the cremation was entirely covered by a heavy earth mantle. This charcoal, C-760, was dated at 219 B.C.±275. From the evidence presented in Libby (1955, p. 99) one might think that the sample from the mound floor should date earlier than that from the top of the mound. Since a full report on this mound has not yet appeared, however, it is too early to judge either the correctness of the radiocarbon dates on the two samples or the type of material which was recovered from this particular structure.

Six of the Adena radiocarbon dates are from the Toepfner Mound near Columbus, Ohio, which was excavated by R. S. Baby for the Ohio State Museum. Two of them are from the University of Chicago laboratory and four are from the University of Michigan. It is of interest to note that charcoal from Feature 2 of the Toepfner Mound was dated as C-923 at 427 B.C.±150, while the same material was dated as M-517 at 350 B.C.±200. These dates, then, are in substantial agreement. The oldest date from the site is from Feature 7 and is C-942 at 830 B.C.±110. The latest date is from Feature 4 and is M-519 at 250 B.C.±200. The range in time suggested by the radiocarbon dates, from 250 B.C. to 830 B.C., seems rather long for the erection of a single mound, even one that does have a number of multiple features. The cultural features from the Toepfner Mound, while not yet completely published, certainly demonstrate that it is relatively early within the Adena cultural sequence. It is not, however, as typologically early as the site on the property of the Dominion Land Company in a suburban area of Columbus, Ohio. This mound was excavated in 1953 by Baby and Goslin (Baby, 1953), and, because of its single post-mold circular house pattern and its unusually heavy thick grit-tempered pottery, with large lug handles somewhat similar to those on stone bowls, it is clearly toward the beginning of the Adena cultural sequence. The site should be one of the earliest in the central Ohio area. In what area in Mexico is such a culture complex known?

James H. Keller has recently dug the Wagner-Merk Mound in the outskirts of Cincinnati for the Cincinnati Natural History Museum. This was a large and complex mound. At the approximate center of the mound and 9 feet above the base and 15 feet below the original upper surface an extended burial had charcoal associated with it. Although the charcoal was about 2 or 3 feet from the burial, judging from the position of the fragmentary log casts, it seems to have resulted from activities associated with the interment. The charcoal itself was in two heavy laminated concentrations and in relatively dry soil. This material has been dated as M-570 at A.D. 90±200 years.

The final Adena mound date is from the Florence Mound in Pickaway County near Fox, Ohio. This mound was dug by Richard G. Morgan for the Ohio State Museum and charcoal from a ceremonial fireplace has been dated as C-874 at A.D. 525±250. During the excavation a circular gorget made from a human skull was found with an infant burial. The gorget, upon which was engraved the head and claws of a raptorial bird, has been illustrated in Webb (1940, p. 126). The style of the drawing resembles that on the Adena tablets and most of these, in turn, resemble the style of art which is common in the Hopewell mounds. Another example of this same art style is the Adena effigy pipe from the Adena mound, which is clearly in a Hopewell style, both in the position or stance of the figurine and the curvilinear decoration on the breechclout. The ear spools of the figure also show similarity with Hopewell.

The total range of the Adena dates is from 830 B.C. to A.D. 782. On the one hand I believe that the dates which are after approximately 200-300 A.D., are too young for the Adena cultural complex; on the other hand, I do not believe that the earliest levels of Adena have yet been dated in the Ohio Valley. On the basis of this belief, then, the Adena culture of the Ohio Valley clearly begins earlier than the Hopewell in both the southern Ohio and the Illinois areas. It is about on the same time level with the Poverty Point development in the Lower Mississippi Valley, if the dates from that site are of the correct order of magnitude.

OHIO HOPEWELL

Unfortunately, we have only four dates from Ohio Hopewell sites. The first, and earliest, of these is on conch shell fragments and is C-137, which is composed of materials from burials No. 260 and 261 in Mound 25, and from other shell fragments of the same species from the same mound. The date on these shell fragments is 335 B.C. ±210 years. The burials were placed in Section 3 and the following information is given in Moorehead (1922) as to the placement and association.

>   Two skeletons, Nos. 260 and 261, lay together near the base line with the heads west. The mass of material deposited with them exceeds that associated with any other burial so far discovered in the United States. The objects were laid so as to form a rectangle 7 feet long and 5 feet wide, and were frequently so closely spaced as to overlap one another. The most remarkable find was a copper celt 22 inches long, which weighed 38 pounds. In spite of its size it was very symmetrical.
>   The objects covering the two skeletons were as follows: Sixty-six copper celts, ranging in length from 1 1/2 to 22 1/2 inches; one stone celt, 11 inches long; twenty-three copper plates, mostly fragmentary, and a great number of pieces; one very large jaw; a curious copper head-ornament; a broken shell; some very fine pearls; pearl and shell beads and teeth; carved bones and bone fragments; effigies; meteoric iron, partly worked copper, etc.; and colored earth. Several other burials were found in Section 3.

The second date is C-139 at 94 B.C.±250. The material on which the run was made was identified as bark from burial No. 248, and was obtained from Section 2 of Moorehead's excavations. He describes this burial as follows:

No. 248 (Cat. No. 40167) lay with the head toward the west. Another skeleton, with its head in the same direction, lay to the west of it. The skeleton, which was badly decayed, was 5 feet 11 inches long. Associated with it were some very remarkable objects. At the right shoulder lay a large platform pipe and a beautiful agate spear-head. A copper plate lay on the breast, and another on the abdomen, while a third lay under the hips. These plates, when lifted, were found to have preserved not only cloth and sinews, but portions of the muscles of the individual. Cut, sawed and split bears' teeth covered the chest and abdomen, and several spool-shaped ornaments and buttons of copper were found among the ribs. The body had apparently been dressed in a cloth garment, extending from the neck to the knees, upon which had been sewn several thousand beads, some of pearl and others of shell. Upon the skirt of the garment had been sewn some of the largest and most beautiful pearl beads found in any of the mounds, together with bears' teeth, etc.

The head had been decorated with a remarkable head dress of wood and copper (Plates XLIX, and Fig. 11). The mass of copper in the centre was originally in the form of a semi-circle reaching from the lower jaw to the crown of the head. It had been crushed flat by the weight of the earth, but part of the original contour was still apparent. The antler-shaped ornaments were made of wood encased in sheets of copper, one-sixteenth of an inch thick. They originally had four prongs of nearly equal length. Willoughby says with reference to this object:—

The carved head-plate had been flattened and broken, and the antlers turned back by the superincumbent weight of the earth. The head-plate was originally of the form illustrated in Fig. 12a, and covered the head from the forehead to the base of the skull, and the branching antlers probably rose perpendicularly. In the construction of the antlers the aboriginal artisan first selected limbs having the proper curve and the required number of branches similarly arranged. These were cut to a suitable form and carefully covered with thin copper. The bases of the antlers were perforated laterally and secured beneath the head-plate.

The third date is C-136, which is dated at 1 B.C.±200 years. Moorehead's description of this altar is given below.

The first altar found was in Section 3, about 28 feet north of the copper find and upon the base line of the mound. It was evident that a quantity of wood had first been placed in the basin of the altar, and that the earth had been heaped over it and the objects, while it was still burning. Thus, although the contents of the altar were badly charred and burned, not all the objects had been destroyed. The objects had been heaped in the cavity of the altar without any regularity of position, and included mica ornaments, spool-shaped copper ornaments, copper balls, many other copper objects, large beads, bear's and panther's teeth, carved bones, several effigies carved out of stone, stone tablets, slate ornaments, beautiful stone and terracotta rings, quartz crystals worked in various forms, flint knives, and cloth. The heat of the fire had evidently been intense for much of the copper was melted and run together.

In other sections of Moorehead's report there are some interesting additional data as to the objects found with Altar 1. There were several effigy forms, including a very fine effigy head which was carved in antler; a remarkable series of stone rings of a specific ear-spool type; quite a number of sandstone tablets of Adena-Hopewell form; stone plummets; a perforated boat stone; a bar amulet, cones of quartz crystal; a quartz core from which flake knives or blades had been removed; one of the best Hopewell plain rocker-stamped vessels from Ohio (Martin, Quimby and Collier, 1947, p. 269); and a fair amount of cord-marked, grit-tempered pottery which is relatively thin.

The artifacts associated with these three radiocarbon dates from Hopewell Mound 25 are among the finest and the most representative of Hopewellian culture that it would be possible to find anywhere. It should be observed that the oldest and the youngest dates from the Hopewell site were obtained from Section 3. It is, unfortunately, impossible at this time to attempt to determine the sequence of construction of Mound 25 or to try to gain some idea as to the probable time order in which the burials and their associated materials were placed in this very large mound. The probabilities are, as Moorehead has suggested, that the mound was built over a period of years and that there may well be a span of two or three generations before this large and complex structure was finally completed.

The complete or almost complete Hopewell plain rocker-stamped vessel, which was found in Altar 1, has plain rocker stamping all over the body of the vessel. Such a style of decoration is late within the Hopewellian sequence in the Illinois Valley. Furthermore, the cord-marked pottery from the altar and from the fill and other locations within Mound 25 is, clearly, most closely associated with the Weaver variant of the Illinois Valley.

The fourth (and last) Ohio Hopewell radiocarbon date was obtained on charcoal from a mound near Rocky Fork Lake, Highland County, Ohio. It was submitted to the University of Michigan laboratory in December, 1956, by Raymond S. Baby of the Ohio State Museum. He described the sample as follows: "The sample consists of charred log around the top edge and charred bark lining from a rectangular sub-floor burial bed beneath the south-central part of the mound. The cremated burial was found deposited on the bottom of the feature." In a subsequent letter Mr. Baby stated that he removed the cremated burial and collected the charcoal sample after the removal of fill earth which had been placed back in the depression by the digger. He thinks that there is no record of artifacts or pottery recovered by the digger, although this is, of course, uncertain. He also said, "It should be noted, however, that earlier explorations (1890's?) of another but smaller mound of the same group revealed classic Hopewellian artifacts—copper breast plate, ear spools, etc., mica and pearl beads." He suggested that the mound was probably late Hopewell. The date for this mound is A.D. 40±200.

I have suggested a number of times before that the Ohio Hopewell pottery complex cannot be derived from the Illinois Valley, nor vice versa (Griffin, 1941; 1945; 1946). In other words, the Ohio ceramic complex is quite distinct, possessing some features derived from the southeast in a notably minor proportion, such as check stamped, complicated stamped, and simple stamped surface finish, which are found at a number of sites; whereas much of the basic general pottery tradition is certainly present in the Ohio area during the early phases of the Adena culture. Some features of the Ohio Hopewell pottery, especially the use of dentate stamping and rocker and rocked dentate stamping, are suggestive of the Point Peninsula ceramic complex in the New York area. The Hopewell Zoned Stamped decorated pottery, however, would seem to have come in from, or at least be at the same age as, that of the Hopewell ceramic group in the Illinois Valley. The general Weaver character of much of the Ohio Hopewell pottery plus the vessel shapes, with vertical to outsloping rims occurring on round-based jars, indicates that the Hopewell pottery in the Ohio area passes into a Late Woodland stage before the development of early Fort Ancient pottery in southern Ohio (Griffin, 1952a). The early Fort Ancient pottery is in turn partly derived from the preceding Late Woodland pottery.

NORTHEASTERN POINT PENINSULA AND EARLY WOODLAND DATES

The Williams Mound is located in Warren County, in northwestern Pennsylvania. The charcoal run from this site came from Pit 2 in a lens 30 to 33 inches below the surface of the mound, and the specimen, M-51, is dated 850 B.C.±300. The site was identified by A. K. Guthe (1950) as Hopewellian, but this identification may not be completely accurate. While some presumptive evidence exists that the burial mounds in this section of Pennsylvania and southwestern New York are primarily Hopewellian, the list of artifacts from the Williams Mound is somewhat less than precisely Hopewellian. Objects recovered include chipped-stone tools, antler tools, an abrading tool, and pottery. Chipped-stone tools were scrapers, drills, projectile points, blades, and flake knives. The projectile points, according to Guthe, are side-notched, corner-notched, and stemmed and are rather thick and crudely fashioned. The blades were varied in shape, and some of them had retouching along one side of the flake. Most of the pottery fragments were from the upper part of the mound. The pottery was crudely tempered and rather coarsely made. Surface finish of the sherds is cord-roughened on both inside and outside and corresponds in that regard to the normal definition of Vinette I. The burial pattern followed by the builders was to dig a number of shallow pits into a ridge which parallels Conewango Creek, then place the burials in the pit and then cover them with dirt. Later a mound about 4 feet high was formed with additional soil obtained from the ridge immediately north of the burial site. It may well be that the top mound fill contains pottery which has nothing to do with the builders of the mound and may be somewhat earlier. On the other hand, on the basis of the type of pottery, steatite bowl fragments, plus other items in the mound, it is difficult to regard the complex as clearly indicative of a Hopewellian occupation, and it might well be slightly earlier than the first appearance of Hopewell in the upper Allegheny drainage.

The Morrow site has a multiple occupation of Point Peninsula and Owasco (Guthe, 1957). It is located in Ontario County, New York, on the northeast side of Honeoye Lake. Excavations during a land-development program revealed a Point Peninsula locus which included bird stones, a pottery tubular-pipe section with expanded bit, cache blades, chipped stone drills, projectile points, copper beads, net sinkers, rectangular and diamond-shaped gorgets, and some pottery which was picked up in the loose dirt which had been moved by power machinery. The pottery would fall within the designation of Vinette I, as it has exterior and interior cord-marked surfaces. The material dated was charcoal from Pit 24 and was found with cremated bones, evidence of a net, and a few chipped stone artifacts. From the materials obtained both W. A. Ritchie and A. K. Guthe are inclined to regard the site as a Point Peninsula II occupation. It was dated as M-640 at 570 B.C.±250.

A burial area at the Oberlander site in central New York has been attributed to the Point Peninsula I occupation and the date, C-192, is 998 B.C.±170. The material was crematory charcoal from burial No. 6 on the Oberlander 2 site. Ritchie (1951) indicates that it is very difficult to tell exactly what the cultural correlation of this date and cremation is to the sequence of materials on the adjoining Vinette site, which develops from Early Woodland up to the Middle Woodland period. The date, however, would suggest that it belongs in the period of almost exclusively Vinette I type of pottery which is found in the deeper zone of the neighboring cultural deposit, which is known as the Vinette habitation station.

The Burley site, northeast of Sarnia, Ontario, and near Port Franks, had in its first level of aboriginal occupation charcoal which was dated at the University of Chicago under their number C-192 at 998 B.C.±220. The pottery from the Burley site points rather clearly to an early stage of the dentate stamp development which appears both in the Illinois Valley as early Hopewell and in the New York area as an attribute of the Point Peninsula II ceramic complex. At the Burley site this pottery is definitely thicker, and the stamped impressions are usually somewhat larger than those in the New York area (Jury, 1952). However, the pottery shows a definite connection with that from the New York area because of the channeled or brushed inner surface, a feature which hardly ever appears on the Hopewellian pottery in the Illinoian area. Unfortunately, there was very little other material in this occupation level, although a number of artifacts of bone and stone were recovered. When this specimen was submitted it was thought to be associated with the early one-outlet stage of the Nipissing Great Lakes, but it is believed at present that this date is associated with the later Algoma stage of Lake Huron.

E. F. Greenman recovered charcoal fragments from a streak of black sand apparently carried by wave action from the bottom of a hearth on the KB-1 site near Little Current, Ontario. At least some part of the occupation at this site may be attributed to a Point Peninsula ceramic complex period, but there is also a ceramic period when the dentate stamp has not appeared. It is not certain to which Woodland culture type this, dated as M-194 at 230 B.C. ±300, belongs. A second date from this site is on beaver fur which was wrapped around copper axes in association with burial No. 8 in 1952. The burial was accompanied by four copper celts with flattened narrowed polls, a large copper four-sided awl or spindle, about 550 small copper beads, and 15 shell beads. The beaver fur has been dated as M-428 at 90 B.C.±200. While no analysis of the cultural complex at this site has been made, the copper celts with the burial would seem to be more closely related to the Hopewellian period than to Early Woodland.

I intentionally do not include the Red Lake site (neé the Hunter site on Red Lake), Jefferson County, New York (Ritchie, 1955) in my northeastern section discussion, because I am confused by a site labeled as Point Peninsula 2 Focus (Libby, 1955, p. 93) or classic Point Peninsula, but which does not have any of the Point Peninsula pottery types or many of the traits associated in my thinking with Point Peninsula. I am also unable to understand why pottery of the Vinette I type which is presumably associated with the Red Lake occupation should be so much earlier than its appearance at the Morrow site (where it is called Point Peninsula II), the Oberlander melange, or in the Orient Focus where it seems to date roughly 1000 B.C. I am puzzled how it is possible to have three separate cultures—Lamoka, Laurentian, and Point Peninsula I—in New York at 2500 B.C. without more evidence of cultural admixture.

ILLINOIS HOPEWELL DATES

In this paper I refer to early, middle, and late Hopewell in the Illinois Valley. These temporal designations are applied to ceramic complexes recovered in stratigraphic position in a number of village sites and to ceramic seriation from Hopewell mounds and villages. A few landmarks in the recognition of this sequence will be presented. In the first detailed presentation of the Woodland occupation in central Illinois, Cole and Deuel (1937, pp. 204-05) recognized a sequence of Black Sand pottery followed by the Morton Focus pottery, which they called the Central Basin phase, and this phase was followed by the Hopewellian phase. As a result of studies of Illinois Hopewell pottery, including the large collection from the Clear Lake site gathered by the late Mr. and Mrs. Schoenbeck of Peoria, Illinois, and the stratigraphic excavations of the Snyders site in Calhoun County, Illinois (Griffin, 1952b; Powell, 1957) made in 1947 and 1948, a sequence was formulated, which has been verified, amplified, and modified by additional studies. Early Hopewell time in Illinois is that period in which the pottery is composed of early forms of the Havana ware group, as in the lower levels of the Snyders site, Havana Mound 6 (Griffin and Morgan, 1941) and the Dickison Camp site (Fowler, 1955, p. 215). The middle Hopewell period is that which sees the introduction of the Hopewell group of pottery—this is the most highly developed and diversified ceramic complex of northern Hopewellian and it coincides with the majority of features which are diagnostic of Hopewellian. The late Hopewell period is equated with the increasing dominance of Weaver utilitarian pottery, the gradual disappearance of the Havana group, and the breakdown of the Hopewell group into the Baehr group. Late Woodland in Illinois follows the disappearance of the Baehr ceramic group and of the diagnostic Hopewellian artifacts.

There are a considerable number of dates from Hopewell village sites and mounds in Illinois. The sequence of many artifact types and of behavior patterns within the Hopewellian culture in Illinois is not clearly understood, but these dates give some valuable suggestions as to the probable time periods of the various cultural units. The radiocarbon dates support the ceramic stratigraphy and provide a chronological framework for it. One of these sites is the Poole site in Pike County, Illinois, which was excavated by John C. McGregor for the University of Illinois. Dr. McGregor believes that the Poole site begins during early middle Hopewell, while my brief examination of some of the pottery suggests that it runs from middle Hopewell to late or even post-Hopewell in time. The first date from this site is M-15 and is on mussel shells from a village site pit. The date on this material is 550 B.C.±300. A somewhat more reliable date from the same site is on charcoal from within a vessel of the type Baehr Brushed, which was in Section 5 and area A-3. This material, M-183, has been dated at A.D. 210±250. The second date I regard as particularly reliable for reasons which are presented later (p. 13).

Salvage operations for the Illinois State Museum by Richard S. MacNeish, during the destruction of a large mound south of Havana in Marion County, Illinois, produced material which has been dated at two laboratories. The sample was from a wood and bark capping on the lower edge of the primary mound. This part of the structure had then been covered by a secondary mound. The Chicago assay on their sample C-152 was 386 B.C.±256, while the University of Michigan, M-20, carbon sample which had been prepared at Chicago was dated at 250 B.C.±250. My interpretation of the pottery inclusive in Mound 9 (McGregor, 1952) is that it is unlikely that Mound 9 is any earlier than middle Hopewell in the Illinois Valley. It is unfortunate that the pottery from the Mound 9 fill was not kept separate in the sherd counts from the material in the village underlying the mound.

The Wilson Mound group in White County, Illinois (Neumann and Fowler, 1952), has had a number of radiocarbon dates made on materials from the subfloor tomb pit in Mound Wh^{o}6. The first of these dates was C-684 and was released to Thorne Deuel as 130 B.C. ±160. Subsequently, this same specimen was given a different acid treatment by the same laboratory and was issued in Libby (1955) as A.D. 1227±180. In an effort to clear up this discrepancy Dr. Deuel very kindly sent to the University of Michigan additional samples from the subfloor tomb of Mound 6 of the Wilson group. The first sample, charcoal from the central tomb, is M-559 and is dated 50 B.C.±200. The second sample, M-558, fragments from antler flaking tools from the subfloor pit, is dated 0 A.D.±200. The subfloor pit was 15 feet long by 11 feet, 8 inches wide, and in its center a sub-subfloor pit 3 feet deep, 2 feet wide, and 5 feet long had been excavated. Four adult males and two females were placed in an extended position around the sides of the large pit, while an elderly female was buried in the smaller pit. There were three other burials in the mound. The three fine effigy platform pipes, the plain platform pipe, copper celt and beads, cut bear jaws, *Busycon*-shell container, carved shell spoons, and the antler drifts indicate that this mound is a fine example of Hopewell burial customs. The deepest burial had only a clam shell and a clay platform pipe with a round platform and cylindrical bowl. No pottery was in the mound. Other mounds of the Wilson group did contain Havana and Hopewell Zoned Stamped pottery, but their age in relation to Mound 6 is a matter of conjecture.

The Rutherford Mound in Hardin County, Illinois (Fowler, 1957), has recently been dated from charcoal taken from an area of fired earth located in the northwestern quadrant of the mound just above the floor. This, M-560, has an age of A.D. 425±200. The pottery complex at the Rutherford site is an interesting one, indeed, because it has a similar ceramic style for late Hopewell in southern Illinois to that of the Illinois Valley. As Fowler has indicated, the vessels at Rutherford correspond to the Weaver pottery of the Illinois Valley and to the broken-down Hopewell rocker stamping which is found over the entire vessel surface and is known to be very late Hopewell in the Illinois area to the north. The single vessel with simple stamp surface finish, which was placed with burial No. 6 in the Rutherford Mound, is very close in most of its features to a vessel from the Meppen site in southern Calhoun County, Illinois. The Meppen pot was associated with a handled mussel-shell spoon, flake knives, and sherds with plain rocker stamping. Small tetrapodal feet, as on these two pots, is of rare occurrence in Illinois, and these vessels and their associations imply that this particular tetrapod form is a trait characteristic of very late Hopewell pottery in Illinois. Another point of similarity to the Rutherford Mound pottery is to be found in the majority of the ceramic complexes of Ohio Hopewell. Here I have been impressed for some time with the general similarity of most of the Ohio pottery to the Weaver-style pottery in Illinois. It is significant that vessels from the base of Mound 25, of the Hopewell group, have this same general Weaver-ware appearance, and that tetrapodal feet of the same small size bunched close together at the base of the vessel are in evidence.[3] From the published illustrations it is clear that some of the pottery from the Turner site near Cincinnati has this same general style of small tetrapod support (Willoughby, 1922, Pl. 24). There are other striking artifacts from Rutherford: three copper conjoined tubes or panpipes, two excellent effigy platform pipes, a plain platform pipe of stone and one of clay, handled mussel-shell spoons, copper ear spools and beads, and a cache of pulley-type ear spools or rings made of pottery, sandstone, cannel coal, and jet. The stone spools are almost identical to those from Mound 25 of the Hopewell group.

In Calhoun County, Illinois, from Mound 8 of the Knight Group, a *Busycon*-shell dipper was cataloged as M-164 with a date of A.D. 250±300. It should be of the same age as the Hopewell material from the mound, including the famous figurines (McKern, Titterington, and Griffin, 1945). Additional burial goods in this mound are three Hopewell Plain vessels, two of which have a crude rim treatment similar to that on the Baehr pottery group; an excellent Baehr Brushed vessel; two Hopewell Zoned plain rocker stamp jars with

---

[3] Many of the sherds from Moorehead's excavation in Mound 25 of the Hopewell site are now in the Museum of Anthropology at the University of Michigan.

wide rocker impressions which cover most of the body; a zoned-punctate vessel of the Baehr group and a crude Pike brushed or scratched jar. The *Busycon*-shell container which was submitted for a radiocarbon date was in an area of limestone slabs, some 12 feet long and 6 feet wide, which were piled up to a depth of 2 feet. Among the slabs were a *Cassis*-shell container, four perforated bear canines, two pearl beads, and a short, straight-sided copper celt bearing a textile impression.

The Steuben site is in Marshall County, Illinois, on the west side of the Illinois River. A fairly large village site is at the base of the bluffs on the flood plain of the Illinois, while a mound group is located directly above on the bluff. Mound Ma^O 202 is the largest mound of the group and is 103 feet long and 38 feet wide. At the time of its excavation by Dr. Dan Morse and his son Dan Morse, from Peoria, this mound had a height of 5 feet 8 inches at its northern end. They determined that it had been originally made up of three small burial mounds which had subsequently been capped to cover all three primary mounds in a single structure. In one section of the mound, Pit D contained a number of burials in association with it. One of the burials, No. 43, was located just to the side of the pit. A section of charred log from alongside it was dated as M-378 with an age of A.D. 290±250. The burial itself, which was also charred, has been dated as M-380 with an age of A.D. 300±250. Because of the presence of Baehr Brushed and Hopewell Zoned rocker stamp of a late variety, the materials included in this Steuben mound suggest that it was erected in middle to late Hopewell times. The village site below these mounds provides evidence, from stratigraphic pits put in by Dan Morse and the University of Michigan, that the Steuben occupation begins in middle Hopewell times with the marker types of Hopewell Zoned dentate stamp and red-filmed, along with the Havana pottery group, and lasts well up into late Hopewell. Weaver pottery is strong in the lower levels of the site and becomes dominant in the upper levels. The distinctive Steuben Punctated is almost the only decorated pottery at the close of the occupation which has Havana ware paste.

The Bedford mound group, Pike County, Illinois, was excavated during the summer of 1955 by Gregory Perino, assisted by Dan Morse for the Gilcrease Foundation of Tulsa, Oklahoma. Through the kindness of the participants the University of Michigan was able to obtain radiocarbon material which helps to place these mounds and their associated materials into the Hopewellian sequence and culture type. Mr. Morse numbered as Mounds 10 and 11 a large earth mound, which had on the base a subfloor log tomb on the north and on the south another log tomb which was placed upon the ground surface. In between these two primary structures there was another log tomb. The logs for this central feature were unusually large, some 2 1/2 to 3 feet in diameter. The large log on the south side of the central feature furnished the material for the M-444 sample, which was dated at 10 A.D.±250. Above this log tomb there had been placed a layer of flat rocks and above it and to one side were crematory remains, including charcoal which was dated as M-443 at 20 A.D.±250. In the subfloor pit tomb to the north of this dated material was an extended female, and in the burial pit were three pottery vessels. One of these is a Hopewell plain bowl, while the other two are Hopewell Zoned rocker dentate stamped. In addition to the vessels associated with this elderly female there were a bone scraper, ten narrow shell spoons, and a plain platform pipe. In the log tomb to the south were three extended female burials, and at the feet of one of them were the skeletal remains of an infant. This tomb contained a long, antler projectile point about 5 inches long, and a plain platform pipe.

In Mound No. 4 of the Bedford group a small subfloor pit had been excavated and it contained a prone female burial. The pit had been capped with a low earth mound and then, in the secondary layer of the mound, a rock crypt constructed which included an extended skeleton with large copper and silver ear spools about 4 1/2 inches in diameter. These ornaments were placed at the ears. To the right and left of the neck were large, cut bear canines, perhaps grizzly bear, which had been inset with pearls. Just above the pelvis was a small copper celt, while around the ankles were strings of *Anculosa* beads. The burial in the rock crypt was an adult male. To the east of the rock crypt and on the same level was an extended adult burial associated with charcoal, and this specimen, M-445, is dated at 230 A.D.±250. Bedford Mound 9 enclosed a log tomb which was placed centrally in the mound on a prepared floor. Charcoal from one of the logs has been dated as M-446 at 400 A.D.±250. In the log tomb there was part of a child skeleton, and additional skeletal material was recovered from the corner of the tomb. The artifacts inside the tomb include fragments of a turtle carapace, a small copper awl, a conch-shell fragment with an engraved bird design, three cut sheets of mica, and shell beads shaped somewhat like the platform of a platform pipe which had been pierced longitudinally. Resting on the upper log along one side of the tomb was a very fine raven effigy platform pipe with a flat base.

The Irving village site is located in Pike County, Illinois, a short distance from the Poole site. It was excavated by John C. McGregor, who assigns the site to very late Hopewell to Late Woodland. My interpretation of the pottery agrees with McGregor's, for it overlaps the late occupation at the Poole site and continues well on into what I would describe as the late Weaver and Jersey Bluff level. Charcoal from square B of this site has been dated as M-489 at A.D. 770±250. This date should apply to the Late Woodland occupation at the Irving site.

Donald Wray of Peoria, Illinois, excavated extensively in the Weaver site in Fulton County, Illinois some years ago, and Richard MacNeish also excavated a number of areas. The MacNeish collection is now in the Museum of Anthropology at the University of Michigan. This site runs from middle Hopewell up to the close of the Hopewell period, when the Weaver pottery is dominant on the site and when the shift from late Hopewell to Late Woodland takes place. Dr. Wray excavated a house site of the Hopewell culture which contained pottery, which was identified by him as 90 per cent Hummel Stamped and 2 per cent "classic" Hopewell. This would mean, in my interpretation, that it belongs in the middle Hopewell period of the Illinois Valley. Freshwater mussel shell from this house site has been dated as M-256 with an age of 350 B.C.±250. It would seem that this date, based on mussel shell, is somewhat too early for the actual age of the middle Hopewell material in the Illinois Valley.

In June and December of 1926, Ernest and Marion Dickson, of Fulton County, Illinois, excavated in Mound F° 77 (Cole and Deuel, pp. 133-36; Dickson, 1956), and uncovered two log tombs which contained Hopewell burials with an extensive amount of grave goods. Don Dickson visited their excavations a number of times and picked up a little wood from the log tombs. He believes that the wood which he gave to me in 1955 was taken from the west or southwest of the two log tombs in Mound F° 77. What little ceramic material was obtained by the University of Chicago in their investigations of the Liverpool area would suggest, because of the predominance of the Naples Dentate Stamped series and Havana Zone Stamped, that the village occupation, presumably accompanying the construction of these mounds, was in the middle Hopewell period in the Illinois Valley. The date, however, for the wood, probably oak, is A.D. 480 ±200. We have another sample of wood from this tomb and will make another run, because this date is somewhat too late by at least three or four hundred years for the included material and for the log tomb construction which was the central feature of the mound.

NORTHERN HOPEWELL AND LATE WOODLAND DATES

Several radiocarbon dates from the northeastern Iowa and southwestern Wisconsin area are pertinent. One of these is from the Sny-McGill mound group in Clayton County, Iowa. Mound 43 was excavated by Paul Beaubien for the National Park Service. A charcoal sample from the east portion of the mound was cataloged as M-305 and dated as 480 B.C.±250. This mound was conical in shape, approximately 78 feet in diameter and 6 feet in height. It contained bundle burials, copper beads, and Red Ocher blades and several layers of red ocher. The charcoal was collected from a partly consumed pole not in close association with the principal inclusions. It must have been in place when the mound was formed. Sherds of a later-day pottery similar to Madison Cord Impressed that were found in the fill closer to the surface than the charcoal and away from the center of the mound, apparently were introduced after the original period of construction. The artifacts collected and illustrated by Beaubien (1953a, p. 60) strongly suggest that the original mound inclusions belong to the Red Ocher culture group of Illinois and are not Hopewell in time. Another date from this same mound is M-308 and was run on charcoal from square 11 L2, 3 to 3 1/2 feet below the mound summit and about 2 feet to 2 1/2 feet below the surface. This specimen was approximately 20 1/2 feet west of the largest charcoal sample from the mound. It also has suggestions, because its age of 550 B.C.±250, that it dates the Red Ocher type of materials which are inclusive in the mound.

In the Effigy Mound National Monument in northeastern Iowa, Mr. Wilfred G. Logan excavated Mound 33, which he interpreted as a Hopewell mound, for it had a rectangular subfloor pit circled by a rock enclosure placed outside the pit on the original bluff top surface. This mound had been excavated previous to Logan's careful excavation. Among the artifacts associated with the mound fill, according to Logan, were a rectangular copper gorget with two holes, tubular copper beads, a pearl bead, a mica fragment, and cremated, extended, flexed and, probably, bundle burials. The charcoal submitted to the University of Michigan came from along the edge of the rock enclosure and was part of a charred log. The radiocarbon date on this sample, M-310, is A.D. 200±300. In the Ph.D. thesis which Mr. Logan completed in January, 1958, he states his belief that a series of northeastern Iowa Hopewell mounds which contain rock alignments and rectangular subfloor pits should be placed in a late Hopewellian period.

Mound 55 of the Effigy Mounds National Monument was excavated by Paul Beaubien. According to his report (Beaubien, 1953b, p. 129), a large mass of charcoal was found in the central area. This mound contained evidence of cremations as well as Hopewellian blades of the Snyders corner-notched type and a bear-canine ornament. The date on the charcoal, M-40, is A.D. 1050±300. Mr. Beaubien joins with me in thinking that this date is not applicable to the Hopewellian material inclusive in the mound. I personally feel that, in view of the concentration of effigy mound occupation in the area, if the date is applicable to the time of the burning of the charcoal, then it refers to an intrusive pit during the Effigy Mound occupation.

Mr. Beaubien also excavated Effigy Mound No. 30, which is interpreted as a bear or buffalo mound with charcoal and a layer of nondescript rocks present. No evidence of a burial was observed during the excavations. The date on this effigy mound, M-41, is A.D. 1080±300. Mound No. 24 of the Sny-McGill group was also excavated by Mr. Beaubien. Included in the materials were cord-impressed pottery belonging to the general Lake Michigan or Effigy Mound group. Mr. Logan, who has examined the pottery, believes that it is clearly related to Weaver cord-marked as far as body treatment is concerned. On the neck area there are rocker dentate stamped impressions. Charcoal from this mound was gathered by assembling small pieces from just below the surface; it was not associated with the mound's intentional inclusions. The date on this sample, M-306, is A.D. 1520±200. Another mound of this same group, No. 27, is a bird effigy, and the charcoal recovered, scattered finds in the mound fill from 6 inches to 1 1/2 feet below the surface, has been dated as M-307 at less than 200 years ago. It is probable that neither of the dates on Mounds 24 and 27 pertain to the initial period of construction of the mounds. Certainly, a date of A.D. 1520 is much too late for the pottery type with rocker stamped material. It should belong to the period of transition from late Hopewell to the Effigy Mound culture in northeastern Iowa.

In Dodge County, Wisconsin, Mr. Warren L. Wittry (1956) excavated Kolterman Mound 18 and interpreted it as an otter mound of the Effigy Mound culture. The charcoal, M-398, dated at A.D. 770±250, is from a cremation in the heart region of this effigy. There was an excellent Madison Cord Impressed type pottery vessel and three chipped stone implements in burial association.

My present interpretation of the Hopewell materials in northeastern Iowa and southwestern Wisconsin is that they do not exhibit the underlying ceramic sequence and other developmental traits which would suggest a gradual development in place. The Hopewell culture of these areas seems to be closely connected with the general Illinois Valley development, with the possible exception of southwestern Wisconsin which does not show a strong development of the Havana Zoned Stamped types. I believe that the specifically Hopewellian complex in these areas spread or moved into the areas during the middle Hopewell period. The marked similarity between the eastern Iowan and Illinois Valley Hopewell could have been the result either of the same groups of peoples using the Illinois and Mississippi valleys at various seasons of the year or of two closely related groups of people participating in a very similar culture pattern. The data from northeastern Iowa now being studied by Logan represents a gradual shift of the late Hopewell into the early Late Woodland and Effigy Mound cultures of the Iowa-Minnesota-Wisconsin-northern Illinois area. One phase of the development in this area, which is associated with late Hopewell, is the appearance of the horizontally cord-impressed decoration on round-bottom, jar-shaped vessels with a constricted shoulder and a vertical to slightly flaring rim. This pottery complex, which is associated with effigy mounds and at least one type of which is the Madison Cord Impressed in the Wisconsin area, seems to move south into the Illinois Valley where it overrides and displaces the late Weaver complex as far south as Beardstown.

The Sorg site is located in Dakota County, Minnesota. Charcoal from this site was submitted by the St. Paul Science Museum through Dr. Elden Johnson to the University of Michigan. The charcoal was gathered from a limestone hearth, Feature 1, at a depth of 21 inches. Although there was no pottery in direct association with it, the hearth was at the level from which the majority of Hopewellian sherds came. Below the hearth a nearly complete Hopewellian vessel was recovered. The date for this sample, M-447, is A.D. 1150±200. I was informed by Mr. Vernon Helmen, who examined the ceramic material from the Sorg site, that there is Late Woodland pottery on this site, and on the basis of other radiocarbon dates it is probable that this particular date belongs with such Late Woodland material rather than with the Hopewellian occupation.

Certain other Late Woodland dates contribute to an understanding of the close of the Hopewellian period. In Muskegon County, Michigan, Edward Gillis and George Davis of Grand Rapids, have in recent years been very carefully digging a small village site. This is a "pure" Late Woodland complex, and from the materials, there is a clear indication that it is relatively early within the Late Woodland period. Charcoal from this site, M-512, is dated at A.D. 960 ±150. Dr. William A. Ritchie has sent in to the University of Michigan a number of samples of Owasco material. Two of the sites which he believes to be Early Owasco have given dates which serve to confirm this interpretation. One of these is from the Snell site in Montgomery County and has a date of A.D. 780±200, while the other, the White site in Chenango County, has a date of A.D. 900 ±250.

HOPEWELL DATES FROM CENTRAL AND WESTERN MISSOURI

Four of the radiocarbon dates are from Hopewellian sites in Missouri. The first of these is from the Wakenda site (McKinney, 1954) in Carroll County. The site is located near the bluff of the north bank of the Missouri River and on the north side of Wakenda Creek. McKinney reports five other Hopewell sites (in this publication) in Carroll and Saline counties within a short distance of the Wakenda site. All of them are ceramically close to the Illinois Valley middle to late Hopewell, for the illustrations given are of the Baehr series, that is, poorly made Hopewell Zoned and Hopewell decorated rim styles along with Havana and Naples stamped varieties. Charcoal from the refuse pits on the north side of the Wakenda site that was associated with Hopewell pottery and other artifacts has been submitted to the University of Michigan and has been dated as M-448 at A.D. 130±250. Among the artifacts are three-quarter grooved, polished and unpolished stone axes; stone and pottery platform pipes, including one with a cylindrical base; flint effigies; and a clay figurine head of the Hopewell style. McKinney refers to six other Hopewell sites in Carroll and Saline counties which he does not describe in his report.

The Renner site in Platte County, Missouri, may be regarded as the type site of the Kansas City Focus (Wedel, 1943). During excavations for a pipe line, J. M. Shippee recovered charcoal from four different pits some 2 to 3 1/2 feet deep in the same excavation trench. This charcoal, M-454, has been dated at A.D. 680±250. The Renner ceramic complex has the highest proportion of plain rocker stamping and plain pottery of any of the Hopewellian sites in the north. Compared with the Illinois Valley Hopewellian sequence, the Renner site belongs toward the end of the latter half of northern Hopewell. Wedel's description of nine other Hopewell village sites in the area suggests that some of them with higher proportions of cord-marked body sherds and dentate stamped decoration may represent a slightly earlier period than does the Renner site. This date of A.D. 680 for the Renner site is probably too late, based on the Illinois Valley chronology. Renner should date about A.D. 200 to 400. We have additional radiocarbon material from the Renner site which was submitted by James Howard.

The above paragraph was written in December, 1957, and the Chronology Chart was prepared in the spring of 1958. During the first two weeks of August, 1958, two samples from Renner have been dated. The first of these is M-571. This charcoal sample is from Level 4, square 70-E-5 (Roedl and Howard, 1957). The date is 1850±200 B.P., or A.D. 108. The second sample, M-572, is also charcoal and is from Pit 7, Level 3, 12-18 inches deep. The date is 1950±250, or A.D. 8. These dates are more nearly in accord with archaeological interpretations than is M-454. The spread from A..D. 8 to 680 is, I believe, a longer life span than is reasonable for the cultural material of Hopewellian nature at Renner. One may, understandably, doubt that there is enough cultural change indicated at Renner to require the passage of some 670 years.

J. M. Shippee excavated in a mound believed to be the Curtiss Mound of the Keller-Brenner group (Wedel, 1943, pp. 154-56). He obtained charcoal from two different areas of the mound. The first sample was from a fire-burned area in the lower levels, and has been dated as M-399 at A.D. 490±250. The second is from deep in the mound and about 2 feet from the fire-burned area, and has been dated as M-400 at A.D. 300±250. One may well doubt that these dates apply to the large blades illustrated by Wedel (1943, Pl. 43). These blades were obtained by Curtiss in mounds near Kansas City and are typical of, and apparently limited to, the Late Archaic to Early Woodland levels in the lower Missouri Valley. The dates may apply to late Hopewell or the Late Woodland occupation which made extensive use of stone slabs in the construction of cairns, vaults, floors, and other features in their burial mounds.

In central Missouri, the Kansas City area, and in northeastern Oklahoma, the Hopewellian occupation is clearly related to that in the Illinois Valley. It seems to begin approximately in the middle phase of Illinois Hopewell and then to pass through somewhat the same sequence of a shift from well-made Havana Zoned dentate and Hopewell decorated pottery into a stage of Woodland pottery which is equivalent to the Weaver and Canteen types in Illinois. We do not have evidence of an Early Woodland complex in this western area which could develop into the local Hopewellian pottery types, whereas such ancestral types are represented in Illinois. This absence of developmental Hopewell suggests diffusion from the Illinois area or, perhaps, even groups of people moving out from that area into the Missouri Valley. Further, the radiocarbon dates indicate that the materials in the lower Missouri Valley are significantly later than some of the earlier Hopewell materials in Illinois. It is probably too early at this time to be dogmatic as to the exact reason for the appearance of these Hopewellian materials to the west. Irrespective of the exact mechanism of origin, however, there does seem to be adequate evidence that the western Hopewellian culture passed gradually into the local Late Woodland units. One phase of this shift, I would think, would be the Sterns Creek pottery complex between Kansas City and Omaha, for it is representative of Late Woodland pottery which bears a striking resemblance to some of the Canteen types of the Cahokia area. Another phase of the shift to Late Woodland would be the Boone Focus of the lower Missouri Valley. One difficulty in shifting populations from the Illinois area to the west is that there does not seem to be a cultural discontinuity in Illinois such as would result if a large segment of the Hopewell population moved away carrying the Hopewell culture with them. There are many evidences that the culture persists with gradual change from late Hopewell into the early Late Woodland ceramics all up and down the Illinois Valley and in fact in southern Illinois as well. If there were a clear and striking break between a good "pure" Hopewell complex in Illinois and the widespread cultures of the succeeding Woodland period, one might assume that there was good proof that the Hopewell people and their culture had spread out in a number of different directions, leaving a vacuum which was filled by the Late Woodland complex of the Illinois area.

THE DATING PROBLEM IN THE LOWER MISSISSIPPI VALLEY

Radiocarbon dates from the Tchefuncte sites in the Lower Mississippi Valley area imply that Tchefuncte is significantly later than the general interpretation which was given to it by scholars in the southeast some years ago. There is now a group of seven radiocarbon dates from sites of the Tchefuncte period. Five of these have been presented in a recent publication by Ford and Webb (1956). The first two Chicago dates run were from the top level of Tchefuncte Midden A, and were measured for C-150 at A.D. 1317±150 and C-151 as A.D. 717±250. Since Tchefuncte Midden A contains both Coles Creek and Marksville material in the top levels of the site (Ford and Quimby, 1945) it may well be that the charcoal and shell from these two areas pertained to these two occupations. Or it may be that the shell date, which is C-151, simply reflects the greater antiquity of some shell specimens over charcoal samples from a comparable level. Deer antlers collected by W. G. McIntire from 30 to 60 inches below the surface at Midden B of the original Tchefuncte site, run as Humble No. 30 on the organic fraction of the antlers, gave a date of 250 B.C. ±110. This would come close to the archaeological estimates of the probable age of the Tchefuncte culture.

W. G. McIntire, of Louisiana State University, obtained *Rangia* shells which were associated with Tchefuncte Plain pottery at a depth of 4 1/2 feet below the mound surface in the Big Oak Island site, New Orleans Parish, Louisiana. These shells, M-243, have been dated at 270 B.C.±200 and are in close association with one phase of the Tchefuncte ceramic culture. According to George I. Quimby, the Big Oak Island is one of the purest of the Tchefuncte sites. The date, within the range of error of the *Rangia* shells, should be valid. Another group of *Rangia* shells, from 3 1/2 feet below the water level on the periphery of the Little Woods site in Orleans Parish, Louisiana, has been dated as M-218 at A.D. 380 ±250. It is significant, perhaps, in this regard that the Little Woods site also contains Marksville and Coles Creek materials (Ford and Quimby, 1945). Hence, it may be that this collection from the periphery of the deposit of the site does not belong specifically to the Tchefuncte stage. There are two other dates, both from *Rangia* shells which were collected by McIntire and are from Tchefuncte period sites in St. Tammany Parish, Louisiana. One of these is H-76, which is dated at A.D. 520±100, and the other is H-28 which is dated at A.D. 50±110.

There have been a series of ten dates from the Poverty Point period of the Lower Mississippi Valley, based on samples from the Jaketown site in Humphries County, Mississippi, and from the Poverty Point site in West Carroll Parish, Louisiana (Ford and Webb,

1956, pp. 121-22). The dates would seem to average around 900 to 400 B.C. for a cultural period in the Lower Mississippi Valley which clearly precedes the Tchefuncte period just as Tchefuncte is clearly earlier than the Marksville to Issaquena levels.

I would tend to agree with Webb and Ford that the Marksville period dates in the lower valley should be slightly earlier than those of the Troyville-Issaquena materials, and that there is probably not much time involved in the occupation of the sites attributed to the specifically Marksville material. It is obvious that we need additional radiocarbon material, preferably charcoal, from sites in Mississippi and Louisiana that can be attributed specifically to the Marksville Focus in the lower valley, so that we can be more certain about the time span of the Marksville complex.

Eleven dates pertain to sites with materials of the Troyville-Issaquena foci in Louisiana and Mississippi (Ford and Webb, 1956, pp. 119-21). They range in age from 530 B.C. ±300 to A.D. 1090 ±100. An examination of these dates and of the materials which were used for dating implies that Troyville and Issaquena probably fall within the period from A.D. 500 to A.D. 900. Seven dates attributable to the Coles Creek period in the Lower Mississippi Valley range from A.D. 400±100 to A.D. 1310±250. The earlier date attributed to Coles Creek is based on *Rangia* shells and would seem to be about 500 years too early. My interpretation is that the Coles Creek time span is roughly from A.D. 900 to somewhere around A.D. 1300.

Radiocarbon dates for the Tchefuncte, Marksville, and Troyville-Issaquena levels in the Lower Mississippi Valley are significantly later than the dates on comparable cultural levels in Illinois, Ohio, and Missouri. The comparable, and sometimes identical, material which is found in the lower valley and in the Ohio to Missouri region is to me a reliable evidence of contemporaneity, and I am puzzled by radiocarbon dates which indicate that such is not the case. The dates suggest that the Marksville period would fall somewhere between 550 and 750 A.D., yet the ceramic materials of the Marksville site, the copper ear spools, the platform pipes, and other items attributable to northern Hopewellian suggest to me that Marksville is on the middle level of Hopewellian development in the Illinois Valley. Some platform pipes and ceramic materials from the Troyville-Issaquena stage indicate essential contemporaneity with the middle to late Hopewell occupation in the Illinois Valley. Dates of A.D. 500 to 900 in the Lower Mississippi Valley do not conform to the Illinois Hopewell dates which cluster between 400 B.C. and A.D. 400. It is difficult to understand why cultural influences from the north should take so long to reach Mississippi and Louisiana or why, if the cultural resemblances are the result of group movement from north to south, it should take so long for groups of people to move from Illinois, into the Lower Mississippi Valley. One of the best cultural indications of probable contemporaneity of Issaquena with Ohio Hopewell is a series of sherds which were kindly sent to me by Dr. Robert Greengo from the Mabin site in Yazoo County, Mississippi. This small group of pottery was stylistically somewhat out of place in the Issaquena Focus and bore a strong resemblance to Havana Zoned Stamped pottery from the Illinois area. The sherds from the Mabin site are significantly thinner than the normal Havana pottery, and, with their clay temper, are clearly distinguishable from the Illinois Valley material. A single date from the Mabin site, H-148, is A.D. 650±100, while most of the Havana Zoned Stamped material from Illinois would date from 1000 to 250 years earlier.

It should be noted that the Poverty Point complex is dated significantly earlier than the Hopewellian complex in the north. It is difficult, therefore, to see how Hopewellian material in the north could be a source for certain features of the Poverty Point complex as Ford has suggested (Ford, Phillips, and Haag, 1955, pp. 145-55). The earliest Adena dates in the Ohio Valley do go back into a period roughly equivalent to Poverty Point, and in Adena one finds the earliest examples of burial mounds in the Ohio Valley and the earliest appearance of earthworks. There are, however, no earthworks in the Ohio Valley that resemble at all closely those at the Poverty Point site. The core and blade industry of Poverty Point is not a significant part of the Adena complex. The microflint specimens of the Poverty Point period are not very similar to the wide variety of core types and the flake knives of Hopewell. In the north it is the Illinois Valley area, not the Ohio center, which seems to have the closest connections with the Hopewellian cultures of the Lower Mississippi Valley, and in the Illinois area there are very few, if any, earthworks comparable either to Ohio, or to Poverty Point.

LITERATURE CITED

Baby, Raymond S.
    1949   Cowan Creek Mound Exploration. Museum Echoes, Ohio State Mus., Vol. 22, No. 7, pp. 54-55.
    1953   Archaeological Field Work, 1953. Ibid., Vol. 26, No. 10, pp. 79-80.

Beaubien, Paul L.
    1953a   Cultural Variation Within Two Woodland Mound Groups of Northeastern Iowa. Amer. Antiq., Vol. 30, No. 1, pp. 56-66.
    1953b   Some Hopewellian Mounds at the Effigy Mounds National Monument, Iowa. Wisconsin Archeologist, Vol. 34, No. 2, pp. 125-38.

Cole, Fay-Cooper, and Thorne Deuel
    1937   Rediscovering Illinois: Archaeological Explorations In and Around Fulton County. Chicago: Univ. Chicago Press.

Crane, H. R.
    1956   University of Michigan Radiocarbon Dates I. Science, Vol. 124, pp. 664-72.

Crane, H. R., and James B. Griffin
    1958a   University of Michigan Radiocarbon Dates II. Science, Vol. 127, pp. 1098-1105.
    1958b   University of Michigan Radiocarbon Dates III. In press.

Dickson, Don F.
    1956   The Liverpool Mounds. Cen. States Archaeol. Journ., Vol. 2, No. 3, pp. 85-92.

Ford, James A., Philip Phillips and William G. Haag
    1955   The Jaketown Site in West-Central Mississippi. Anthropol. Papers, Amer. Mus. Nat. Hist., Vol. 45, Pt. 1.

Ford, James A., and George I. Quimby
    1945   The Tchefuncte Culture, an Early Occupation of the Lower Mississippi Valley. Mem. Soc. Amer. Archaeol., No. 1.

Ford, James A., and Clarence H. Webb
    1956   Poverty Point, a Late Archaic Site in Louisiana. Anthropol. Papers Amer. Mus. Nat. Hist., Vol. 46, Pt. 1.

Fowler, Melvin L.
    1955   Ware Groupings and Decorations of Woodland Ceramics in Illinois. Amer. Antiq., Vol. 20, No. 3, pp. 213-25.
    1957   Rutherford Mound, Hardin County, Illinois. Scientific Papers, Illinois State Mus., Vol. 7, No. 1, pp. 1-44.

Griffin, James B.
    1941   Additional Hopewell Material From Illinois. Indiana Prehist. Res. Ser., Vol. 2, No. 3, pp. 165-223.
    1945   The Ceramic Affiliations of the Ohio Valley Adena Culture, In The Adena People, by William S. Webb and Charles E. Snow. Univ. Kentucky Repts. Anthropol. and Archaeol., Vol. 6, pp. 220-46.

Griffin, James B.
  1946 Cultural Change and Continuity in Eastern United States Archaeology. *In* Man in Northeastern North America. Papers Robert S. Peabody Foundation Archaeol., Vol. 3.
  1951 Some Adena and Hopewell Radiocarbon Dates. *In* Radiocarbon Dating. Mem. Society Amer. Archaeol., No. 8, pp. 26-29.
  1952a The Late Prehistoric Cultures of the Ohio Valley. Ohio State Archaeol. and Hist. Quart., Vol. 61, No. 2, pp. 186-95.
  1952b A Preview of the Ceramic Relationship of the Snyders Site, Calhoun County, Illinois. In The Snyders Site, Calhoun County, Illinois. The Greater St. Louis Archaeol. Society, pp. 14-21.
  1952c Archeology of Eastern United States. Chicago: Univ. Chicago Press.

Griffin, James B., and R. S. Morgan, eds.
  1941 Contributions to the Archaeology of the Illinois River Valley. Trans. Amer. Philos. Soc., Vol. 30, Pt. 1. Phila.

Guthe, Alfred K.
  1950 Archaeological Field Work—1950. Rochester Mus. of Arts and Sciences, Mus. Serv. Bull., October, 1950.
  1957 Our Investigation of the Past Is Continued. *Ibid.*, October, 1957.

Jury, Wilfred and Elsie
  1952 The Burley Site. Univ. of Western Ontario Mus. of Indian Archaeol. and Pioneer Life, Bull., No. 9.

Libby, Willard F.
  1955 Radiocarbon Dating. 2d Ed.; Chicago: Univ. Chicago Press.

Martin, P. S., G. I. Quimby, and Donald Collier
  1947 Indians Before Columbus. Chicago: Univ. Chicago Press.

McGregor, John C.
  1952 The Havana Site. *In* Hopewellian Communities in Illinois, edited by Thorne Deuel. Scientific Papers, Illinois State Mus., Vol. 5, pp. 43-92.

McKern, W. C., P. F. Titterington and James B. Griffin
  1945 Painted Pottery Figurines from Illinois. Amer. Antiq., Vol. 10, No. 3, pp. 295-302.

McKinney, Joe J.
  1954 Hopewell Sites in the Big Bend Area of Central Missouri. Missouri Archaeologist, Vol. 16, No. 1.

Moorehead, Warren K.
  1922 The Hopewell Mound Group of Ohio. Field Mus. Nat. Hist. Publ., 211, Anthropol. Ser., Vol. 6, No. 5.

Neumann, Georg K., and Melvin L. Fowler
  1952 Hopewellian Sites in the Lower Wabash Valley. *In* Hopewellian Communities in Illinois, edited by Thorne Deuel. Scientific Papers, Illinois State Mus., Vol. 5, pp. 175-248.

Powell, B. Bruce
  1957 Hopewellian Pottery of the Lower Illinois Valley: The Snyders Site Ceramics. Papers Mich. Acad. Sci., Arts and Letters, Vol. 42 (1956), pp. 219-24.

Ritchie, William A.
  1951   A Current Synthesis of New York Prehistory. Amer. Antiq.,
         Vol. 17, No. 2, pp. 130-35.
  1955   Recent Discoveries Suggesting an Early Woodland Burial Cult in
         the Northeast. New York State Mus. and Sci. Serv., Circ. 40.
         Albany.
Roedl, Leo J., and James H. Howard
  1957   Archaeological Investigations at the Renner Site. Missouri Archaeologist, Vol. 19, Nos. 1-2, pp. 53-88.
Webb, William S.
  1940   The Wright Mounds, Sites 6 and 7, Montgomery County, Kentucky. Univ. Kentucky Repts. Anthropol., Vol. 5, No. 1.
Webb, William S., Henry A. Carey and Charles E. Snow
  1941   Mt. Horeb Earthworks Site 1 and the Drake Mound, Site 11, Fayette County, Kentucky. Univ. Kentucky Repts. Anthropol. and Archaeol., Vol. 5, No. 2.
Wedel, Waldo R.
  1943   Archeological Investigations in Platte and Clay Counties, Missouri. U.S. Nat. Mus., Bull. 183.
Willoughby, Charles C.
  1922   The Turner Group of Earthworks, Hamilton County, Ohio. Papers Peabody Mus. Amer. Archaeol. and Ethnol., Harvard Univ., Vol. 8, No. 3.
Wittry, Warren L.
  1956   Kolterman Mound 18 Radiocarbon Date. Wisconsin Archeologist, Vol. 37, No. 4, pp. 133-34.

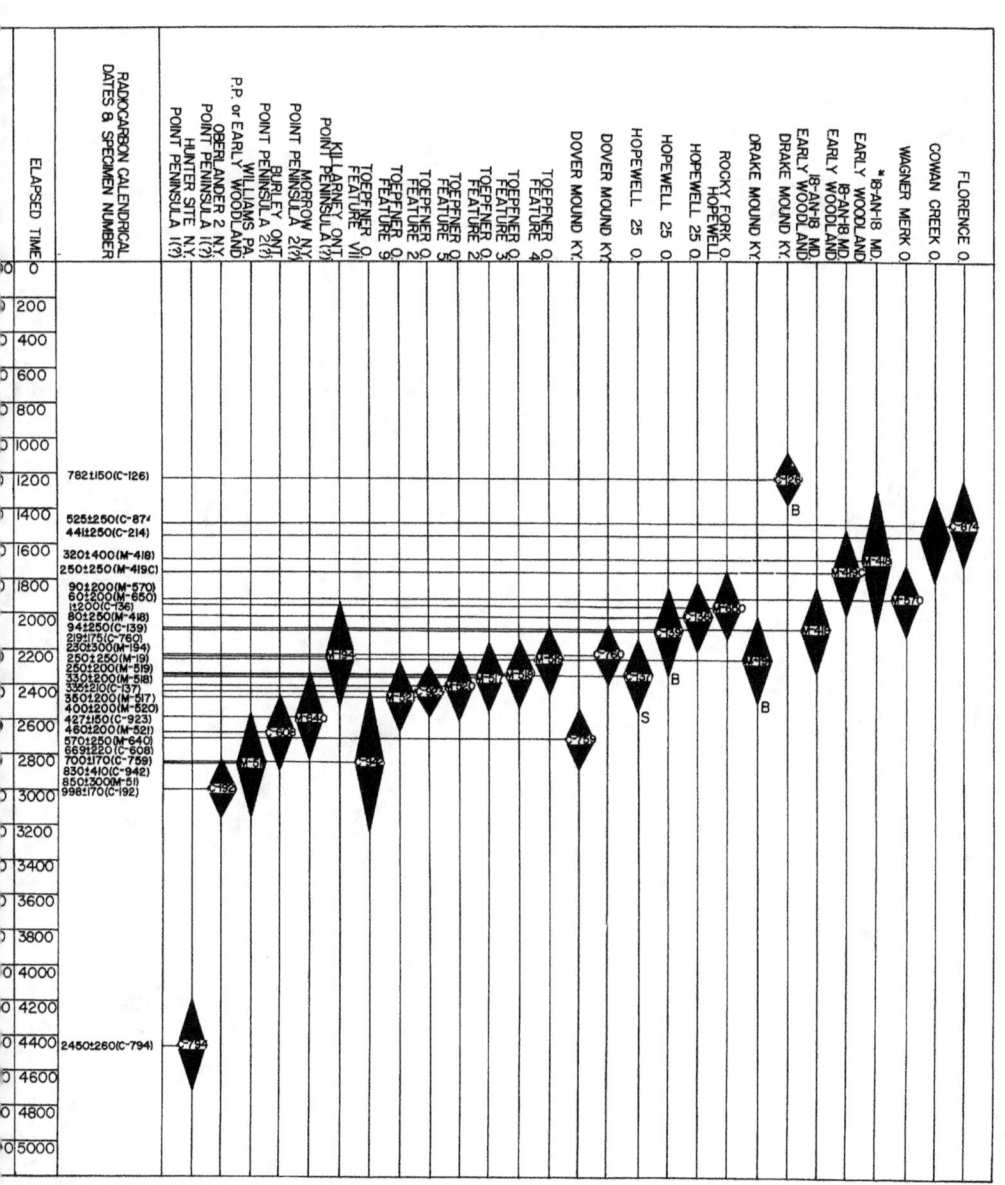

Early Woodland, Adena, and Ohio Hopewell Dates. Unless otherwise noted all specimens are charcoal; S= Conch Shell, B= Bark. *Earlier for specimen M-418 considered more reliable.

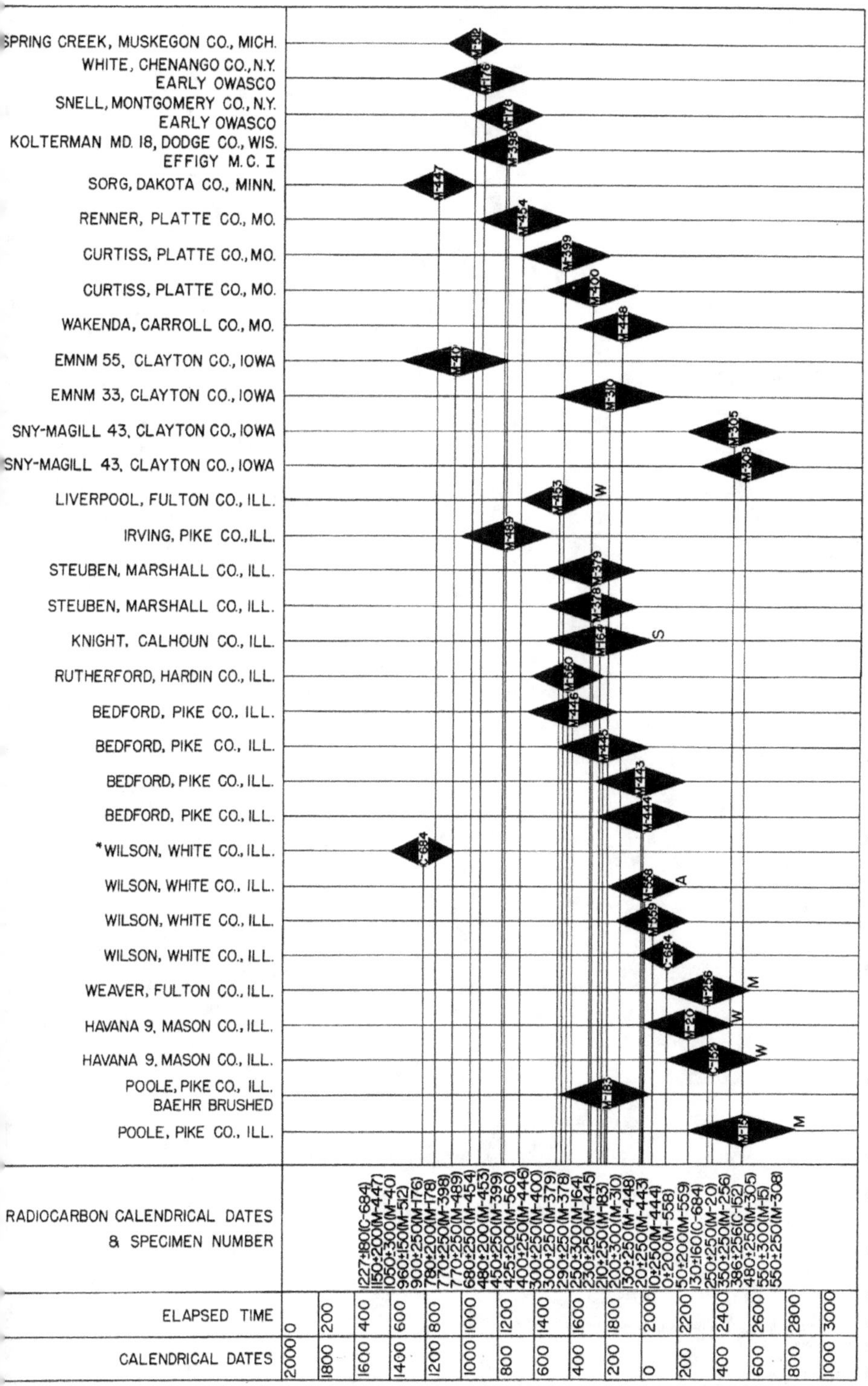

Fig. 2. Northern Hopewellian Dates and some Late Woodland Dates. *Sample run twice. Unless otherwise noted all specimens are charcoal; A=Antler, M=Mussel shell, S=Conch shell, W=Wood.

www.ingramcontent.com/pod-product-compliance
Lightning Source LLC
LaVergne TN
LVHW021232180326
833917LV00012B/396